TOR

Exactly How to Remain Invisible on the Anonymous Deep Web

Joshua Cody

Table of Contents

EXPLORING THE DEEP WEB CAN
BE DANGEROUS

The author and publisher of this book highly discourage you from using TOR for <u>any</u> type of illegal purposes.

Illegal practices are not only highly immoral and damaging to yourself and others, but will also lead you to be punished by law.

The environment of TOR might seduce you to get involved with illegal practices because of anonymity. You also might encounter highly disturbing content on the deep web, which can be accessed using TOR. The simple act of viewing some of this content can already be punishable by law and could cause you to be jailed.

Be aware of this at all times and avoid illegality <u>at all costs</u>, both for your own safety and for the safety of others. Use TOR software at your own risk.

Introduction

The Internet is non-arguably one of the most amazing developments in human history. The worldwide network of computers has forever changed our perception of communication. It started as an innovative development in a laboratory to interchange text messages.

Can you imagine that? During its early stages, the Internet only had code and plain text; no images, no multimedia, nothing else than text. Almost 30 years later, the web has completely changed at a hectic pace. Nowadays, the Internet contains vital information of every user. It carries our personal information, photographs, videos, and much more. Data you may never realize you were creating is floating in the cyberspace as you read these pages, such as your search preferences, cookies, latest search engine enquiries, and so on.

So, the Internet is unsafe not only due to the malicious users who try to grab your personal information for their perverse purposes (such as PIN Codes for credit cards; a risk you should never underestimate) but also due to the personal information ongoing "leakage" that occurs during the regular use of the online services. Do you agree with this manipulation of your personal data?

Most likely, you don't. However, it is rather difficult to escape completely from this exposure. After all, every time you use a certain software tool or a web application; you must agree with the terms of use. Otherwise, you will not be making any use of those services. So, when you open a browser to surf the Internet, you agree with the use of your personal information on the developers' side. For instance, Google collects data from all of us, ranging from locations to personal searches.

Doesn't it sound good? Fortunately, there are more secure options our there; the major candidate in the search engines sector is DuckDuckGo: a search engine that does not store personal information form users. However, as you may already realize, most people will continue to make use of Google. Why? There are two strong reasons. On one side, the risk is not that high and, most likely, people do not care.

Most of us may have been using the worldwide network for quite some time. Have you ever been hacked? And, if so, was it your fault or you just run into a god-like hacker who broke every security protocol until the greenish "Access Granted" message prompted on top of a black screen? If you think it was the latter; you may have watched too many films about cyber-hacking experts who do not actually exist.

Let us face reality for a moment before we resume the course of the book. Just a few, a really small minority of us, will ever be subjected to online threats. And no, I am not talking about that message that shows up on your browser claiming that a virus will destroy the PC, the city and every inhabitant unless you – casually – pay some money. That's just a joke – a disgusting one the first time you run into it.

We will discuss how to avoid such kind of situations and how to handle them when they show up. They will eventually show up as long you continue to navigate online. Just a few of us will lose money due to online hackers. And, among those unfortunate ones, most of them will have made a major mistake – such as forgetting to log out of your Facebook account in a public PC. Has it happened to you? A friend of mine suffered the consequences of such innocent mistake. It didn't have major consequences but it could have.

Just as you do in real life, you should never expose personal data online. Never, ever. So, if you have been hacked, was it the hacker's skill or your "own" fault? I'm not trying to blame anyone; these situations happen. The purpose of this book is to illustrate you in the techniques of becoming a ninja online: someone who navigates and is not seen. And, above all, you will learn many strategies I've gathered during the years to stay safe online.

The ultimate tool we will review is The Onion Routine Project (TOR). Originally developed by the military, The Onion Routine Project was born in a Naval Research Laboratory. Nowadays, fortunately, this amazing software tool is of regular use; and it is open to anyone on the Internet. It allows you to become invisible in your daily navigation. Hence, TOR will be helpful to reduce the risk of data leakage to zero as long as you stick to the recommended use.

Let us start our journey to become savvy navigators and develop a set of practices to enforce the security of your personal info.

Why Is TOR A Viable Solution?

As we have already noted, TOR is the short name for The Onion Router. Its original development by the military meant to establish a safe communication network for government purposes. Nowadays, the TOR servers allow any user to become anonymous online. Just as the peels of an onion (the symbol of TOR), this service has several layers (routers) to move the traffic in order to disguise your real identity.

So, whoever wants to find out your identity while using TOR will run into a bunch of random TOR servers; which, of course, means nothing. The main purpose for this traffic deviation is that the nodes in the TOR network serve to camouflage the real source of the activity (you). Hence, you will be able to stay hidden from the third-party services that track personal information.

What Are the Uses of TOR?

To add some context to this versatile software tool, these are some of the cases where TOR could become handy:

- You want to search some information but you ARE NOT supposed to be doing that. Hence, you need to stay anonymous.
- You want to make us of a public PC making sure to avoid any personal data leakage.
- You do not want to share personal activity online with advertisers, ISPs, websites, and similar data collecting sources.
- You need to dodge the police or state censorship (most likely in countries with such policies), or wish to share knowledge with an organization such as WikiLeaks.

Making TOR Work Properly

The following guidelines describe the DOs that will make your experience with TOR most satisfying:

- **Install TOR browser.** Getting the TOR browser in Windows is quite straightforward. You just need to open the TOR Browser Official Download page, find the latest version and follow the instructions to complete the installation. I will explain this process in detail in Appendix A. In other OS, you need to follow specific instructions according to your system. In the same appendix, I will include some references for the most common cases.

- **Do not use Torrents with TOR.** The TOR network is not meant to be used with peer-to-peer connections for file sharing. Hence, you will be making a poor use of the service and slowing everyone else's connection in the network while doing so. Moreover, BitTorrent exposes your IP address; hence, you will be revealing your ID by using P2P making TOR worthless.

- **Do not allow browser plug-ins.** Have you developed the plug-ins personally? Most likely, you have not. Hence, you DO NOT know if the software tool collects information of your ID during its normal use. Hence, allowing any of such programs to run freely is a risk for your anonymity.

- **Use HTTPS.** The node exits from the TOR network are the most vulnerable points for your anonymity. TOR encrypts the information within its network and camouflages the source of your activity. However, the activity outside the network is exposed. What can you do about it? Make a consistent use of end-to-end encryption, such as SSL or TLS. The possibility of using HTTPS all the time is assured by simply switching HTTPS Everywhere add-on or a similar one in a supported website. Those websites which do not allow HTTPS navigation may expose your activity.

- **Never open downloaded document via TOR while surfing online.** So, imagine you just downloaded a document while using TOR. Now, you – innocently – click on the document's name to take a look. What happens? Most likely, the browser will open a supported document in a separate tab. Most of these documents tend to be shared by Google Drive or similar storage services... which REQUIRE a user account login. So, you will be surfing anonymously and saying "Hey, I'm John Sanders" at the same time. See, the inconsistency? Solution: DO NOT click on stuff that opens more stuff when using TOR.

- **Use bridges.** What do you do in real life when there is a river and you badly want to cross it without touching the water? You sail a boat! Ok, not the answer I was looking for... most of the time, you may walk to a bridge and make use of it to get to the other side. The idea is pretty much the same when you navigate with TOR; you make us of bridges (relays = safe passages) to get rid of censure. The Tor Project Organization also provides a number of bridges for users. These are safe passages to navigate online without compromising your ID. So, make a consistent use of those.
- **Recruit more users.** To become a valuable member of the TOR community, do not surf alone. Call some friends; tell them about TOR. Remember that the more we are online in TOR, the stronger the network will become slowly but steadily.

When Not To Use TOR?

Staying anonymous is not the same as being safe online. After all, the TOR network is far from being the perfect solution for very case scenario; it is a project still in development. To make use of TOR, you need a browser with this protocol. The protocol has not been broken yet but the browser is the weakest link here.

A browser is a program that interacts with the user and the online network. Unfortunately, it is subjected to exploits that someone else may profit. Recently, it was announced that the NSA is able to unveil the user behind the TOR network. Of course, you cannot bet your chances to escape authorities with the use of this network.

Hence, illegal uses are not "safer" or out of the radar when you activate TOR. You just make it harder for the authorities to reach you; and they will succeed eventually. TOR is not a tool to become a criminal; it must not be used for illegal purposes. The incorrect manipulation of the network jeopardizes the TOR community worldwide.

This list summarizes some not recommended uses of TOR:

- **Large file anonymous downloading.** Reason: you will most likely use P2P such as Torrent. Hence, you will be slowing down everyone's connection not to get any benefit, i.e. the authorities will be able to track your download record.

- **Attempting to avoid surveillance from the NSA.** Reason: do not try this. It's not effective this way. Just, don't.

- **"Securing" your online activity in social networks.** Reason: it is a logical inconsistency to make use of services that require your ID and to try to stay anonymous at the same time, don't you think? Plus, you will not be any safer while doing so; you will be equally exposed to the service exploits.

- **You should not try to access official sites (governmental or similar).** Reason: every person who requests such services needs identification.

- **Illegal uses** (children's pornography, unauthorized purchases, drug-related commerce, etc.). Obvious reasons: morally incorrectness & prosecution. Whilst these uses are common for obvious reasons, they are illegal and could lead you to be prosecuted and jailed without warning. TOR's environment makes it very easy to use the browser for these purposes, but these were not the intended uses for TOR.

As you can see, there are several scenarios where TOR is the solution for your concerns. However, in some cases it is not advisable to be using this service so as not to attract unnecessary attention from the authorities; provided that the NSA and the FBI watch any suspicious behavior in this network. A responsible use of TOR is always advised and it is your own responsibility. Let us review how this whole server network works with more detail.

How Does TOR Work?

An onion has multiple layers that protect - and form – the vegetable. Likewise, TOR is a network made of several routers that serve as "layers". Just as in the real case counterpart, the outer layers protects the interior, in your case your identity. Behold the vegetable that inspires TOR anonymity service:

Imagine you need to send a package with some valuable content. How can you protect this item for the delivery? You may grab some bubble wrapping plastic to cover the item. Then, you may add some extra layers to ensure its integrity.

TOR works in a similar way. Your precious item is your personal data plus the inquiries you send to the

Internet. To avoid being tracked easily, TOR directs the flow of information through various points of its network. It is the equivalent of having several layers to protect your ID online. The nodes of the network are made of routers and servers throughout the world.

Does it sound simple? Fortunately, you do not need the technical specifications to make use of the service. Now, let us analyze the security level of TOR.

How Secure Is TOR?

There is nothing 100% secure in life. Not even living under a huge stone could make you completely safe from the outer world threats.

Hence, there is no reason to believe that TOR is any safer than other alternatives in every case scenario. Although it, indeed, excels in regular uses, several weaknesses have been exposed during the years.

This list summarizes some of the exploits that involve TOR:

- ✓ **Autonomous system (AS) Eavesdropping.** Anyone could be spying the traffic that come in and out of the TOR network. With some sophisticated tracking, they could pinpoint your ID or location. Of course, this not possible unless you really are a pro in the hacking strategies.
- ✓ **Exit node eavesdropping.** An exit node is a point where TOR has no longer control of the information sent to a server, i.e. it connects to any computer in the world. Hence, an expert can retrieve passwords, e-mail accounts, and the like from these points. Of course, if you do not use any of those inside TOR, you are safe and sound.
- ✓ **Traffic analysis attack.** Although this kind of attack does not reveal the ID, they could gather some information about the user inside the TOR network. Not a huge concern, though.
- ✓ **TOR exit node block.** Some websites ban TOR users to prevent from accessing their services without identifying themselves. Hence, you will not be able to edit the Wikipedia while using TOR, use the BBC online player, and so on.

- ✓ **Bad apple attack.** This vulnerability relies in exploiting weak services, such as P2P BitTorrent clients inside TOR. Hence, do not make use of such connections to "download" anonymously; you will be jeopardizing your anonymity instead.

- ✓ **Protocols that expose IP addresses.** Other than BitTorrent, there are more protocols which expose the IP address (and, hence, your real ID), such as P2P tracker communication, distributed hash tables, etc. These attacks are focused in the man in the middle vulnerabilities.

- ✓ **Sniper attacks.** What is worse than a denial of service (DDoS) attack? The distributed counterpart; a DDoS, i.e. a group attack to the exit nodes so that the attacker can tell which ones you are using. This works in a "simple" way: you block a large enough amount of nodes so that a user of TOR will have to rely in one of the few that remain operative. What do you get? A higher likelihood to pinpoint the nodes "you" are using; hence, more chance to find out who you are. Of course, this is not precisely a layman's technique.

- ✓ **Heart bleed bug.** This bug reveled and compromised passwords in April 2014 inside the

TOR network. Those protocols were soon deactivated. However, there is a chance of having similar vulnerabilities in the future, although not high. The main premise to avoid such issues it to rely in hidden services; we will review some of them later in this book.

- ✓ **Mouse fingerprinting.** This one is a bit too twisted but it works. Comparing the clicks you make in a website with JavaScript to track mouse movements, an expert proved that is it "feasible" to determine a person's ID. Fortunately, if you do not use public PCs, this risk is not a threat.

- ✓ **Circuit fingerprinting attack.** There were partially unveiled news of a vulnerability related to fingerprints inside the TOR network. Hence, you should better not user bio trackers.

- ✓ **Volume information. The** anonymity that TOR offers you cannot hide the data volume that you move around. Hence, if you are under surveillance of any kind, they could track your steps even with the use of TOR.

- ✓ **Other.** More exploits will continue to appear related as time goes on. Some of them will be immediately solved; others will last longer but will be sidestepped in some manner. Of course, there is nothing like an all-rounder never-exploited system to protect your ID online; just as happens in real life.

The list may seem a deterrent to make regular use of TOR but it is not the case. However, showing the possible risks is part of my duty in this introduction to the service. The moral of the story is this: TOR does not make your online activity 100% secure; it creates anonymity.

This step is rather simple. To make use of TOR you need a browser compatible with the service. You may go to the TOR Project website to download the latest release of this software tool.

In particular, you may be interested in making use of the TOR browser; which is probably the all-rounder alternative to get started in the anonymity online. There are also add-ons for other popular browsers, such as Mozilla Firefox.

If you are a Mozilla user already, this option may be of your interest. Of course, the functionalities are somewhat limited compared to having the TOR browser; but the simplicity of installing an add-on is unpaired. If you like to know the pros and cons of both options, here you have some hints.

TOR Browser Positives and Negatives

These are the most remarkable advantages and disadvantages related to using TOR to navigate.

Upsides of TOR

- **Most reliable anonymity features.** This is a great network to have your ID hidden for most purposes and web activity normal uses; such as simply browsing around to read news without leaving "tracks" behind.

- **Access into Deep Web (or Dark Web).** A juicy but dangerous zone of the Internet. This "place" is not covered by search engines – hence, it is in the dark. Moreover, illegal activities take place in this online "black hole". You should be very careful about what you do and where you surf while in this place – otherwise, you may have trouble with authorities.

- **Most novice "hackers" won't see you.** TOR instantly grants you with a reliable protection from those who have seen too many hacking series or films. They will not touch you BUT a real hacker very well could. So, do not think you are 100% safe.

- **More.** TOR sets a standard for private browsing, it is portable, the access is hidden through .onion sites.

Downsides of TOR

- **Performance is not for picky people.**
  Although the performance has improved in the past few years; it is not precisely like browsing normally. However, there must be a price to pay for such additional anonymity layer, don't you think?

- **You are not 100% secure or unseen.**
  Authorities are watching you. Do not forget that. NSA and FBI take this anonymous activity very seriously. If you end up in illegal-related websites too often or just by chance in Dark Web; they will find you. Avoid those by all means. However, do not be afraid, if you commit a mistake (i.e. enter an illegal website by accident) and you act correctly (A. Immediately exit or B. Report the site), there is no further issue on your side. There is nothing to hide, either. Of course, they may ask you some questions. Paraphrasing ol' uncle Ben "great power demands great responsibility". So, it's always your choice to do the right thing as a citizen.

- **Reputation.** All the previous issues with authorities due to the misuse of TOR lead us to this point. Unfortunately, the TOR community has a toll on its back. However, it is a double-edged sword; it has become very popular among journalists and activists worldwide. There is always room for valuable contributions from the use of TOR.

- **Low latency.** This is a really common issue in the TOR network. So, you'd better be patient. He who is patient shall find what he seeks.

Mozilla Add-on Positives and Negatives

These are the most remarkable features of using the Mozilla add-on version of the TOR service. Let's go over them so you can decide for yourself if it's worthwhile for you.

Upsides of Mozilla Add-on

- **Free open source community.** All the Mozilla products have a public license. Hence, any developer may contribute to the improvement of the service. Moreover, anyone can make sure that the service REALLY provides what it claims.

Transparency is a key factor in the open source communities.

- **Customization.** Just as it is usual in Mozilla, you are able to customize the add-on according to your preferences. Hence, you will have a completely unique browsing experience.

- **Community support.** Most users prefer this TOR version of the service; especially Mozilla supporters. Mozilla Firefox is an all-rounder solid browser that is highly compatible with most devices and OSs. So, if you change your device in the future, it won't affect your experience too seriously. Moreover, the community support is always a plus.

- **More.** There is a large list of features worth noting, such as strong ongoing development, solid HTML5 support, syncs for devices , tagging bookmarks, distraction-free reader mode to enhance the scanning, auto updates, Quick bookmark management, lowest memory & CPU load , integration with Pocket to save pages on the go.

Downsides of Mozilla Add-on

- **Installing extensions demands restart.** This is a pesky situation provided that not every extension support non-restart running. Hence, you'd better be patient about it.

- **Slow performance in some OSs.** Apparently, users point out that the performance in OS X is much slower than that in Windows or Linux. So, be wary if you are a Mac user.

- **Extensions durability is at the stake.** An extension life is an unveiled mystery in Firefox. What happens is that Firefox has its own pace and the extensions have theirs. Hence, it could happen that a given extension is left behind and becomes useless because it is deprecated. So, when you rely in an extension to enhance your experience, also consider the activity of the developers in the updates.

- **More.** There some other disadvantages to using Firefox for TOR navigation but they are mostly situational (i.e. they only affect a minority of users in some case scenarios). For instance, there is enterprise support. You may ignore this if you are an individual browsing from home. Moreover, there is no HDiDPI support; in those High-Res screens the icons look blurry. Unless you are browsing in a 4K screen, you won't notice.

How to Get Started

So, now you have either a TOR browser of the add-on counterpart at your disposal – or maybe both of them! It is time to try some basic online tasks to see the difference from browsing without anonymous features.

In the next section, we will have an overview on the most suitable candidate for the TOR services. Read that section in detail to understand what you should expect from this service and what not to expect. Always make a responsible use of this amazing tool.

Are You A Suitable User For TOR?

We have already stated that TOR is not for everyone out there. I believe that the best way to understand who TOR is meant for relies in reviewing the most recommended practices that are compatible with this service. Let us take a look at the top DOs to become a successful TOR user.

This chapter considers some of the most relevant security-oriented and anonymity-friendly practices for online users.

Change Your Operative System (OS)

"Winbugs" exploits are somewhat legendary. The most widely used OS in the world was designed to be user friendly. Hence, vulnerabilities have not been avoided. Changing to another OS may sound radical but in the long term, you may learn that the benefits are considerable. Linux systems are completely compatible with TOR. In fact, there are some distributions that are TOR-configured, such as Tails and Whonix. Mac is also compatible with TOR, you just need to install the browser and you are good to go; it is also more secure than Windows.

Be Updated

In any case, regardless the OS you are using, keep your system updated. This point should not be overlooked provided that old releases have exploits widely known by malicious hackers. Hence, keep everything as updated as possible; your OS and the TOR browser.

HTTPS Everywhere

You may wonder how to use https in a website that only offers http version. Well, fortunately, there is a solution named HTTPS Everywhere. The supported websites automatically change to HTTPS-mode browsing with the use of this add-on.

Encrypt Your Data

So, why bother being anonymous online if you do not profit from extra security layers like an onion – ring a bell? LUKS and TrueCrypt are two software tools which allow encryption in Linux systems. The more encryption, the more security.

Be Careful with TOR Bundle

Contrary to common belief, the use of this bundle may be counterproductive. Yes, you do add an extra layer but there are vulnerabilities that have been exposed by the FBI. Be careful with overusing these tools.

Disable Java Script, Flash & Java

These disgusting scripts may share your personal information without letting you any chance to avoid it. So, just turn those off to enjoy the surfing experience with more anonymity.

No P2P

It must be the third time I mention this but it is a vital point. If you make use of peer-to-peer connections, you are exposing yourself.

No Cookies & Local Data

Add-ons like Self-Destructing Cookies will automatically delete those undesired bits of information. They may store personal data; so you will be more anonymous without any of them.

No Real E-mail

Never, ever, make us of real accounts of your own with TOR. Otherwise, you will be telling people "Hey, hello World. I'm anonymous. Signature: John Smith." See the issue?

No Google

The most popular search engine in the world actively collects personal data. So, you will be safer using another search engine, like DuckDuckGo or StartPage.

Comply With Legislation

Last but not least, comply with regulations and legislation while surfing online. The NSA and the FBI are watching everyday 24/7 to find out who is making an incorrect use of any service of this kind. You better not draw unnecessary attention in this regard by complying 100% with regulations.

Of course, if you are side-stepping prohibitions from your government, keep your tracks as anonymous as possible. You may only rely in hidden services to establish secure channels for communication, send files anonymously, and the like. Probably one of the safest ways to make use of TOR is to check news without interacting with any website, service, etc. If you are choosing this path, keep in mind that the less interaction you have with the websites, the stealthier you will become.

Moving on to the next section, now we will learn about the kind of information you will browse around while surfing inside TOR. Take a close look at the wide range of possibilities that this network puts at your disposal; starting with the Hidden Wiki.

First Steps with TOR

By this time, you have already opted for one option, either the TOR browser or the Mozilla add-on counterpart, to navigate anonymously. You also know the risks and the benefits that this online ninja-like activity implies.

Hence, it is time to discover exactly what you can do with your brand new anonymous status. When you run the TOR browser, the feeling is like that of launching a smoke bomb the ninjas do in the films.

Become a Ninja

You may wonder what to do inside TOR now that you have logged out of every other application (to prevent them any data sharing). These are the most recommended first steps inside Deep Web.

Hidden Wiki

This website has a similar layout than the Wikipedia; it is the TOR counterpart. There, you can browse the categories of your interest to sort out the preferences you may have. The Hidden Wiki is the place where all the .onion sites on the Deep Web are listed, about all sorts of topics. Finding the Hidden Wiki is simple, just type it into DuckDuckGo Search Engine using TOR and you're only one click away from accessing this Wiki-hub.

You may find a rather large list of websites here, such as:

• **Introduction Points.** These are the most common websites users can access in the first place when they start the TOR browser. Most of the time, you arrive at these site with StarPage, an in-built search engine for TOR.

• **News.** This is one of the main reasons to make use of TOR. You may sidestep governmental bans, censorship and prohibitions to check the international news without restriction. There are portals inside TOR to keep track of the latest news; check those which are updated frequently.

• **History.** Contrary to common belief, History is not taught the same way in every country. Moreover, there are nations which alter real historical events according to personal beliefs, political interests, and so on. Hence, just as happens with news, TOR offers an unbiased version of the facts.

• **Commercial Services.** Do you want to purchase an item without revealing your ID? Of course, there may be simpler ways. However, the rise of the Bitcoins makes it possible to purchase items as anonymously as possible in the online community. Of course, you may be discovered if someone tracks your steps but it will be harder to do so inside TOR in a general basis.

• **Forums.** Do you want to discuss matter anonymously? There are apps which offer this service, such as the Q&A community that Quora currently has in English and Spanish. There, you can post a question and reply anonymously for the community; the developers know who you are, of course. However, if you want to go one step further covering your personal info, you may consider using forums inside TOR and hidden services.

• **Other "dangerous" topics**, such as Hack, Phreak, Anarchy, Warez, Virus, and Crack, etc. Try to avoid any possibly illegal website while you surf inside TOR. In some cases, the websites may pop up without you being able to prevent it. However, paying attention to the information around is the only reliable way to sidestep those sources of illegal activities as much as possible. You may not be able to avoid pop-ups, but you can close them instantly without interacting, right? The same principle applies to the regular use of the Internet.

The main directory of websites inside TOR is the Hidden Wiki. Although the websites lists in the Hidden Wiki may not always be updated; given that some of them may be offline a while ago, it is still a viable source of onion addresses. Keep in mind that the durability of websites inside TOR is more volatile than in the more accessible side of the Internet.

Once you find some websites of your interest, I recommend you to bookmark them carefully. Unlike in regular browsing, TOR URLs are nearly impossible to memorize. Moreover, directories may change drastically all of a sudden forcing you to search thoroughly for a while. The smart use of bookmarks will always be a reliable source of addresses on your side.

Onion Chat

There are also chat rooms that support anonymous communication, known as OnionChat. They are supported by the TOR service so that the availability of the service is more long-lasting. If you happen to have any friends using TOR, you may use these chats as a means of communication.

After all, why bother being anonymous if you are not going to commit 100% to this status, right? Using nicknames is a common practice while chatting in TOR. Never use real life names.

New Yorker Strongbox

This is a website for secure transmissions that writers use to send messages or files to New Yorker's editorial staff. It is anonymous. You will be given a codename when you access so as to never reveal personal information on your side. Most bloggers who maintain websites in TOR network hardly ever post; so you may not get new feeds from those you like to read on this zone of the worldwide web.

Other relevant mentions

Unfortunately, TOR is not a tool that everyone masters right now. Once you are inside the Deep Web, you are completely free. Hence, the sensation of loneliness is more enhanced than when you navigate normally. Moreover, the rather short mean life of the websites does not precisely help to make this sensation any less notorious.

So, when you search for information with TOR, the rule number one is to be patient. The seemingly omnipresence of the low latency in the service also demands more perseverance than usual. The starting point is the Hidden Wiki; a sort of unofficial must-read directory where you can always get some fresh ideas to plan the navigation. Then, you access one website; check the content, click some links, and so on. Of course, you should stay away from suspicious sources at all times.

Tips and Tricks

In this section, I summarize some handy every day's practices that will complement the regular use of TOR for navigation and communication purposes.

Safe Browsing

Keep in mind that TOR is only as effective as your surfing habits are regarding personal ID anonymity. By default, TOR DOES NOT connect to Google. The most famous search engine worldwide is a sewer for the personal information; it gathers extensive logs of everything you search with the service. Instead, TOR connects to "Start Page" a mediator between you and Google; so that the session is completely unidentified. By using Start Page as a relay you assure that your searches are not attributed – or traceable - to your source of activity; i.e. you. At least, not by any simple means; I disregard NSA level of inspection for this observation.

TOR is unable to control the behavior of extension, scripts and websites. Hence, the best way to sidestep those potential risks is to prevent any from taking place. By default, TOR browser does not allow such activity. It is not advisable to change this setting in any moment of your navigation to avoid unnecessary exposure.

Do you know you can view streaming anonymously? Although it may not work every time; YouTube now has a HTML5 beta service running. The default flash videos of this famous website are not available while using TOR due to security vulnerabilities in Flash protocols. Hence, you may not enjoy the experience just as much as in normal surfing mode.

Last but not least, TOR will warn you about documents and files that could potentially disclose information about your ID – either casually or purposely. It is recommended to take a close look at such warnings; you will find that it is not worthy to take any chances.

Anonymous Messaging

In normal navigation mode, there is nothing like anonymous messages. Every messaging client you may think of has monitoring logs of your "private" chats – such as, Google chats, Facebook, Skype, and the like. So, how can we escape "Big Brother" for a moment just to send some undisclosed messages?

Fortunately, TorChat enables just that. You may use this anonymous chat app even in the form of an extension. To make use of this service, go to the official site for the service and download the zip folder. There, you will find an executable to run the application.

This chat client works just as any other messaging program; you will find the layout very intuitive. A remarkable difference from regular messaging clients is that you will be represented by a random set of characters instead of having your real name in the service. Fortunately, you can rename your contacts to

make it simpler to establish conversations –
codenames are recommended. Moreover, as the
service runs in TOR background; nobody within the
network will be able to determine who you are
messaging with at any given moment.

Crypto Messaging

If you want to go one step further, you may try
cryptographic messages via TOR. However, these
services do not run in the background as the previous
one. The strong side is that the messages – although
intercepted – are harder to decipher per se. One of the
common choices is "Cryptocat", which available in its
official website.

Anonymous E-mail

So, what about e-mails? Sending unidentified
messages is acceptable but sometime you may need to
send an e-mail instead. Among the "hidden services"
available in TOR, there is, of course, the e-mail.
However, note that any hidden service IS ONLY

available inside TOR; it may not exist the network without compromising ID information.

To make use of TOR mail, you just need to open the website of this service from within the TOR network. Follow the instructions to sing up and get started.

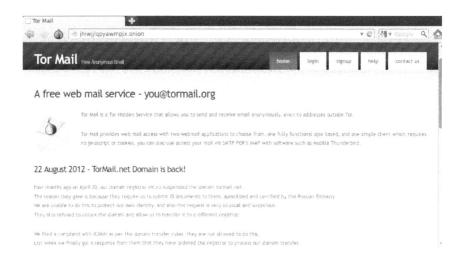

The main advantage of such service is that it cannot be searched of accessed from outside the TOR network. The layout is not very different from that of Gmail and Yahoo mail, so you will find it very intuitive. However, there's much more to do and to discover on the deep web that can be of use. That's what we will be covering in the next chapters. We will also take a look at how to use the deep web to our advantage, as well as what its contents will develop into, when looking into the future.

The Deep Web

We will discuss more about hidden services in this section. Moreover, another review about limitations and security concerns will take place.

Hidden Services

We have already talked about the most common hidden services that users like to consider inside TOR. As you read these lines, more of these services are being developed and some other become deprecated; the Deep Web is in constant change.

Why use hidden services?

Using a hidden service in TOR is a perfect solution to privacy issues because it is never exposed to outer spying (from the regular Internet). So, such services are not taken down, or blocked. Regular Internet services can be easily denied.

Let us analyze this with a simple example. I could very well send massive packets of data to my neighbor's router to deny him access to the Internet, due to saturation. In other words, I can interfere in the communication between the router and the PC my neighbor is using. But I don't, I am a good neighbor!

However, if my neighbor wanted to keep a service in private, connecting two PCs at their place, a wire would suffice to prevent any intervention from outside the home. Simply turn off the Wi-Fi. See where I am going?

Likewise, regular Internet service can be denied rather "easily" – you may need thousands of PCs to deny an official site but the principle is the same: spam. In-home connections are like the TOR network, simply because you can't deny anonymous onion servers. Hence, you can read the TOR e-mail or make use of the private chat every day. Also, people like to use anonymous services to transfer their cryptocurrencies, such as the infamous Bitcoins.

Using bookmarks

Using bookmarks consistently is a skill you need while surfing in the Deep Web. Keep in mind that a typical link in TOR network looks like this:

http://[bunch of random characters here].onion

In other words, it is nearly impossible to remember websites or services addresses in TOR due to the random characters in the URLs. Hence, bookmarks are your best friends to navigate as you like to do.

There is no Google in the Deep Web nor are the pages indexed by regular search engines. So, how can you find information there?

TorSearch

This service is the equivalent of Google inside TOR; but without consistently grabbing personal information from your side with every search. This service is based in the same principle that Google search engine has.

With the inclusion of TorSearch, the traffic volume rapidly increased in the network. Nowadays, it has improved a great deal since the first stages. It is much simpler than ever to find a given hidden service, website, and basically anything you'd like to locate in the Deep Web.

Of course, the hidden Wiki remains as a reference for anyone who want to browse the categories to find one's own interests. This website is moderated to only show public and "acceptable" content for every public.

Limitations, hazards and other issues to consider

Although TOR offers a great solution for online anonymity, it is not exempt of vulnerabilities. Provided that the TOR browser is a modified version of the Mozilla Firefox counterpart, the same exploits could potentially be applicable. Plus, you are also exposed to Trojans, even if you make use of regular browsing. After all, you never know when and where you will come across a virus, right?

Another drawback when you use the TOR browser, is that you will draw the attention of the NSA and maybe other similar governmental agency. They are able to track your activity to reconstruct your steps online. Hence, you really need to be careful about your clicks while surfing. Even showing up in an illegal-related websites may cause you some issues with the authorities. Watch out, you have been warned.

Websites to be wary about

Other than the Hidden Wiki, you also have search engines for products inside TOR. However, you should be wary about scams of any kind. You may want to keep away from some of those search engines to avoid issue with the authorities, such as Grams, a famous website that has gained momentum inside TOR. This search engine is like a replica of Google which is connected with drugs crypto-markets. Hence, watch out if you try to find an item with that tool.

As for online markets, you have Middle Earth, Agora and Evolution, among others. Although Middle Earth offers more functionality in its platform, the counterparts overwhelm the market. The reason behind this success on Agora and Evolution's side relies in a stronger reliability of their services; which is a huge asset inside the Deep Web.

Before purchasing inside TOR, make sure you understand the process and comprehend the service/item you are getting; and its possible repercussions – if there are any. Moreover, be careful about the payment method; you will never want to expose your personal data. If you are able to get some Bitcoins, that is the safest way to purchase in TOR.

Last but not least, read references of a service before making a final decision. Users have very active communities in some websites. Of course, if you are unable to find enough information about a service or website; avoid making use of their offers.

More security concerns about the content

Surfing inside TOR can be potentially more dangerous than doing so in the regular web. In this section, we carry out a security analysis of the kind of content you may find inside TOR network.

• **Dynamic content.** This kind of sites requires queries or forms while you navigate. You will need some experience with domains to browse these websites.

• **Unlinked content.** These websites are not indexed by search engines. Moreover, there are no backlinks or in-links on those sites.

• **Private webs.** Websites which require a login to be accessible. Be careful about potential private data vulnerabilities or fake logins that could make you reveal personal information about you.

• **Contextual webs.** The access context for this websites may vary. For instance, they may rely in previous clients.

• **Limited access content.** These sites implement robot exclusion standards, CAPTCHAs, and the like. Hence, they avoid being indexed by search engines systematically.

• **Scripted content.** This kind of websites demands links produced with JavaScript or another software clients, such as Flash, Ajax, and related.

• **Software.** Apps or programs are required to access these kinds of websites.

• **Web archives.** Some archives allow you to check an old version of other websites. They store these older versions for future checks.

As you can see, the content show up in different formats online either in regular browsing just as it happens in TOR. Hence, being able to tell the difference is important to understand how secure a websites or a service can be. In a general basis, avoid installing programs or running executables you find randomly online so as to minimize the risks.

Future of the Deep Web

Unfortunately, it had to be the recent political instability in the Middle East one of the main reasons to boost the use of TOR. In the past few years, the possible used for this software and network have been shown consistently. People have evaded the censorship from their governments for a large number of reasons – in some cases, just to see cat videos online in Facebook.

However, there is much more than that in the Deep Web. In fact, nobody can tell how much information is stored inside the Deep Web; the section of the Internet that is not indexed by search engines. Some years ago, TOR was estimated to have a few Petabytes of information.

However, this amount may have skyrocketed in the past few years. There could possibly be tenfold, a hundredfold; or even more than those initial estimations.

You can see for yourself – in the last section of the appendix of this book – how easy it is to create one's own server in TOR. It is no longer rocket science; just a layman's procedure right now. There are tons of tutorials you may consult to come up with one hidden service of your own. Just as you are able to do it, so are people from all over the world. This is why the content in TOR is growing exponentially. Users appreciate the benefits of anonymous interactions online so as to feel the – sometimes unjustified – sense of security.

Never forget that TOR does not really protect you any more than the Firefox browser. The same exploits may potentially be applicable to both services in a given moment. Moreover, as popularity remains as high regarding the use of TOR, more hackers may attempt to grab personal information inside the network for malicious means.

Hence, it is a place to be wary about. The Deep Web is not as gentle, content-wise and scam-wise, as the regular counterpart. It's like the real world, but without any rules or supervision.

That is a concern, provided that you already know how "simple" it is to come across scammers online. There are tons of websites that try to induce you to make wrong decisions with your money; ending up in you wasting dollars in vain in most cases. This jeopardizes the reliability of honest vendors. However, that is how the Internet is; that will not change in the foreseeable future.

Does that mean you may not use the WWW? Of course, it does not. You also have a risk of suffering an accident whenever you leave home – or even at home. Applying the same biased logic, you should just stay in bed to be "safer".

I work online every day. I have been doing so for over a decade; I will be doing so in a decade from now. You know what? I cannot wait to see how one of the most amazing developments in human history evolves in the next few years; the Internet has made our lived completely different.

Imagine how communications were half a century ago, remember how they are now. Remember how purchasing was before the Internet, you had to be in person in every shop until you found the precious item you wanted. Imagine how driving was a while ago, no GPS; just you and the road; and, possibly a map.

Privacy Concerns

Now, we read news from all over the globe in an instant, maintain live communications, attend videoconferences, etc. In such a landscape, it is conceivable to need some privacy, right? Hence, TOR was created.

An undeniable amount of people have used TOR to become activists and a part of the anonymous opposing party's forces. Keep in mind than in some countries incompliance with certain censor laws may suppose prosecution and even imprisonment. Hence, using TOR has become a must-do for those who do not want to be oppressed. Moreover, TOR enables private communication at a nearly zero cost; you just need to install the software. It is clear that the use of the Deep Web for various purposes will continue to grow in the foreseeable future. Once you enter the Internet, there is coming back. It is a never-ending source of information that – in the right hands – can be used to boost anyone's knowledge.

Although there are a large number of people using TOR for illegal activities, the community will keep expanding non-stop. In the regular counterpart of the Internet, people also made fraudulent uses; this has never been a reason to banish its use. Authorities need to establish legislation according to enforce a responsible use of these hidden services and the overall TOR network.

Regulation needs to evolve to cover the possible misuse of the Deep Web. In most countries, they have barely focused in this concern. However, the Internet moves at a hectic pace; governments need to stay updated in the matter. Hopefully, in some years the authorities will become more concerned about being updated to the latest in the legislation of the new technologies. Ideally, every time a new development is approved to be distributed, the laws should be able to regulate every possible use people could make. You can see why this is a huge challenge. After all, who could have imagined some years ago the current uses of the Deep Web, right? Sometimes, there is no alternative but to adapt on the go to the latest innovations.

Appendix

In this section, I will guide you in the installation of TOR browser step by step. It's an optional technical read that will help you get started with the software.

Installation of the TOR Browser in Windows 10

This section has a detailed guide to install the TOR Browser in Windows 10. Follow these steps to get access to this browser in no time.

1. Go to the TOR Project website or simply search the latest version of this browser, currently version 6.5 for Windows 10, 8, 7, Vista and XP. On the official TOR Project, click the Download tab at the top right of the site. From the search results, click the link to the official site; you will arrive at the download page.

2. Next, you should select your OS. As you can appreciate, the TOR browser is available for Windows 10, Apple OS X, Linux, Smartphones and in Source Code. Yes, you read it right; you can also make use of this amazing anonymity software tool in your favorite device.

3. Then, choose your language to download the correct version of the installer. In the same page, you can download the TOR Bundle, which is the ultimate set of tools to enhance privacy while you navigate online.

4. Now, you will need to choose the path to save the installer in your PC. Keep in mind that this will not affect the next steps of the process by any means.

5. Once the executable download is finished, click on it to access directly. Otherwise, you will need to execute the installer from the path you had previously chosen.

6. Pick the language for the program and click OK.

7. Choose an adequate path to save the program files; you can also select a secondary hard drive or another memory, such a SD card. Make sure there is enough space for the installation (the executable shows the available and necessary memory).

8. Be patient until the installation is complete.

9. Creating a start menu and a desktop shortcut is the common choice. You will be able to run the browser immediately once the installation finishes.

How to Use TOR with a Firefox Proxy: BlackBelt Privacy

This section explains how to make use of your current Firefox installation to navigate inside TOR with the aid of BlackBelt.

1. Go to this site to download the latest release of this software tool. It's a rather small download which will take a few minutes at most.

2. Once you open the executable, you will be asked to pick the kind of use you will be making for this installation. The options are the following:

   a. **Bridge Relay Operator.** To use TOR and help people remain anonymous while relaying to your computer.

b. **TOR client only Operator.** You just want to make use of TOR without becoming a relay yourself.

c. **Censored user.** If censorship applies to the Internet in your country, choose this option.

3. After choosing the correct option for your profile as a TOR user, you will only need to proceed with the installation.

4. Once the BlackBelt installation is complete, you are ready to browse the Internet. Everything should be ready for you to navigate anonymously now.

Manual configuration

In the case the previous configuration does not function properly, you can easily set up the TOR proxy for Mozilla within a few minutes. These are the steps to take:

1. First of all, you will need to have the TOR browser installed in your computer. However, we are going to make use of Firefox Mozilla for the navigation.

The reason behind this choice is straightforward: Mozilla is a browser with a higher rate of updates than the TOR counterpart. Mozilla developers are more active; hence, they set updates more often. This improves the security of this browser.

2. Then, you open Mozilla Firefox; go to settings, proxy settings.

3. In Windows, follow this path: Menu > Options > Advance > Network > Settings.

4. Now, you just need to set up the proxies manually:
   - **SOCKS Host:** 127.0.0.1
   - **Port box:** 9150
   - Select SOCKs v5 if available
   - Make sure you have "Remote DNS" check marked
   - After No Proxy for introduce: 127.0.0.1

5. Check if TOR works. You will get a congratulation messages stating you are surfing anonymously. Otherwise, you will be notified that your IP is visible. If the proxy does not work, deactivate it until you troubleshoot the issue.

Setting up Hidden Services

Do you know what could be better than using any hidden service in TOR? Setting up yours! It is possible, and not so overwhelmingly difficult, to create your own hidden service. For instance, check this website out to see how a real hidden service is established. Of course, you first need to have the TOR browser installed.

Setting up the local server

1. TOR recommends Savant (for Windows) and the "thttpd Web server" in Mac OS X, Linux and other Unix-based Oss, as the web server to create hidden services in the network. You may use another one under your own risk of vulnerabilities implied.
2. When you open the configuration go to HTTP, then Server DNS, type "localhost". Type "80" in the "Port # To Serve From" box just below.
3. The common path in Windows for Savant homepage is this:

C:\Savant\Root directory

Make sure your "index.html" document is replacing the one that Savant used by default inside this directory in the path.

4. To check that everything is running correctly, you just need to type localhost in the browser address bar. If you want to use another port, other than # 80, then type localhost:[#of the port], for instance, localhost:100 for port # 100.
5. So far, we have the local server online.

Setting up the hidden service

Now, you just need to make TOR know about the new web server you have set up. Follow these steps to accomplish the goal:

1. Close TOR browser if it is running.
2. You need to search for the "torrc" file; you may use the search tool in your computer. You may also find it in this path:

Browser\Data\Tor directory

3. When you locate this file, open it with a plain text editor, such as Notepad or similar. You will need to add some lines to this document, like these ones:

 # Hidden Service

HiddenServiceDir
C:\Users\Name\tor_service

HiddenServicePort 80
127.0.0.1:80

4. You need to change the *C:\Users\Name\tor_service* string for a real path in your computer. Do not select your website as a directory in this case. The last number of the above string must be the # of the port you picked for the web server; in this case, 80.
5. Create the tor_service folder in the case it didn't exist yet. Save and restart TOR browser.
6. Have a look at the message log just to check if there were not errors in the configuration.

7. Inside this folder, you will now see 2 documents: *hostname* and *private_key*. They serve to assure the correct function of your service; protect the key no matter what. Someone else could delete your hidden service with that key.

8. Inside hostname, you will have the onion address of your hidden service. Open this document to read the address and share it with other people.

9. Now, you just need to post anything in this brand-new TOR website. Do not forget that the visitors will have to use TOR to access it.

As you can see, setting up services inside TOR is not that hard. Hence, you will be able to post news, information and share it with any user inside the network. It is that simple to get started in the website managing inside this net. Of course, you may need to master the basics of HTML and CSS to create elegant designs.

Fortunately, there are tons of tutorials out there on how to create websites. Moreover, there are samples online all over the Internet. You may get started with a simple template that you can customize at will.

Happy surfing!

Parting Words

Exploring the deep web is an adventure in itself, but TOR is so much more than that. This remarkable piece of free software allows for communication in ways we didn't expect were ever possible, but in some cases highly needed.

Just imagine being in a country where free speech is oppressed, and not having the means to let the world know about it. And that's just one of the many ways TOR can be used.

Hopefully, this short introductory guidebook on TOR has allowed you to gain some understanding of its uses, possibilities and brought you one step closer to a world in which privacy is respected.

Make sure to keep an eye out for some of the hacking-related books I'm about to publish in the near future.

Joshua Cody

Author & Ethical Hacker

www.ingramcontent.com/pod-product-compliance
Lightning Source LLC
Chambersburg PA
CBHW061027050326
40689CB00012B/2724